First Facts®

A CAT'S VIEW OF THE WORLD

by FLORA BRETT

CAPSTONE PRESS
a capstone imprint

First Facts are published by Capstone Press,
1710 Roe Crest Drive, North Mankato, Minnesota 56003
www.capstonepub.com

LIBRARY OF CONGRESS CATALOGING-IN-PUBLICATION DATA

Cataloging-in-publication information is on file with the Library of Congress.
ISBN 978-1-4914-5050-5 (library hardcover)
ISBN 978-1-4914-5088-8 (eBook PDF)

EDITORIAL CREDITS

Carrie Braulick Sheely, editor; Tracy Davies McCabe, designer;
Katy LaVigne, production specialist

PHOTO CREDITS

Capstone Studio: Karon Dubke, 5, 19; Newscom: Photoshot/NHPA/Yves Lanceau, 21;
Shutterstock: Artmim, cover, 1, Ermolaev Alexander, 17, Grey Carnation, 15, IcemanJ,
7, Nailia Schwarz, 13, Rita Kochmarjova, 4, Steve Collender, 11, Willyam Bradberry, 9
Design Element: Shutterstock; Lorelyn Medina

Printed in China by Nordica
0415/CA21500544
042015   008845NORDF15

TABLE OF CONTENTS

WILD ROOTS

Meow wow! Can you believe today's house cats have **ancestors** from ancient Egypt? We enjoyed getting food and attention from people 4,000 years ago. And we still love to snuggle with our owners today!

Even though we're **domestic** and much smaller, we're related to wild cats. These big cats include lions, tigers, and cougars.

Most cats have tails that are about 9 inches (23 centimeters) long.

ancestor—a family member who lived a long time ago

domestic—tame; no longer wild

5

THE CLAWS COME OUT

We are incredible climbers! Our sharp, curved **claws** help us climb. We keep our claws sharp by scratching them on scratching posts inside or trees outside. Scratching also lets us stretch our leg muscles. If you provide safe things to scratch, we won't ruin your furniture!

We may mark our **territory** by scratching. **Glands** on the bottom of our paws leave scents for other cats to smell.

claw—a hard, curved nail on the foot of an animal

territory—an area of land that an animal claims as its own to live in

gland—an organ in the body that makes natural chemicals or helps substances leave the body

AMAZING ABILITIES

Our abilities set us apart from other pets. We land on our feet almost every time we jump or fall. How? Our tails help us balance and move weight around. We have **flexible** spines to wiggle into tight spots.

Super **sensitive** whiskers help us know if a spot is big enough to fit through. They also help us feel in the dark. Our whiskers are so sensitive that we don't like to have them touched.

We can jump five or six times our body length!

flexible—able to bend

sensitive—able to feel things easily

PINPOINT HEARING AND SUPER SIGHT

These furry ears have a greater **range** of hearing than people's ears. We can hear sounds that are really low and really high in **pitch**.

Our eyes view the world differently from yours. Our eyes see **depth** and movement easily. We can see everywhere but behind us. We can see very well with little light. In the dark our **pupils** open wider to let in more light.

Our ears turn in a half circle toward sounds.

range—the distance from which sound can be heard

pitch—how high or low a sound is

depth—distance from top to bottom or from front to back

pupil—the round, dark center of the eye that lets in light

11

THE NOSE KNOWS

We sniff a lot! Smells teach us about our surroundings. We'll sniff your shoes and pants to see who you've been around. Smells make us want to eat and tell us if food is safe to eat. A stuffy nose becomes dangerous if it makes us stop eating. I'll need to see a **veterinarian** if I get that sick.

A cat's sense of smell is almost 15 times stronger than a human's!

veterinarian—a doctor who treats sick or injured animals; veterinarians also help animals stay healthy

13

CAT CHAT

Purrrrr. That's one way I **communicate**! Sometimes you can hear my low, rumbling purr. Maybe you have felt my body **vibrate**. We purr when we're happy, scared, hungry, and hurt. Kittens purr when being fed. Mother cats purr when **nursing** their kittens.

I also use my voice to show my feelings. My wide variety of vocal sounds can include soft chirps or loud meows. I may hiss when I'm angry.

I'm also communicating when I rub my face on people or things. I leave my scent to mark where I've been and to tell other cats that's my territory!

communicate—to pass along thoughts, feelings, or information

vibrate—to move back and forth quickly

nurse—to feed young with milk from the mother's body

15

ALONE TIME AND PLAY TIME

We're **solitary** animals that nap a lot and play alone often. But we still like getting attention and play time from our owners! I count on my owner to feed, **groom**, and care for me. This **routine** makes me feel safe.

Yawn! We sleep about 17 hours every day. We often nap in warm places, such as on a sunny windowsill.

solitary—living or spending a lot of time alone

groom—to clean and make an animal look neat

routine—a regular way or pattern of doing tasks

CAT CARE

I'm easy to care for. Feed me cat food to keep me healthy. Be sure I always have fresh water to drink. Brush me to remove extra fur and prevent **hairballs**. Clip my nails, and clean my **litter** box daily. Take me to the veterinarian for yearly checkups and **vaccinations**. With good care I can enjoy many happy years with you.

hairball— a ball of fur that lodges in a cat's stomach; hairballs are made of fur swallowed by a cat as it grooms itself

litter—small bits of clay or other material used to absorb the waste of cats and other animals

vaccination—a shot of medicine that protects animals from a disease

I don't need baths. My rough tongue does a good job of removing dirt from my fur.

19

AMAZING BUT TRUE!

Not all cats have tails. The Manx breed may be born without one. But all Manx have at least one **gene** for a tail. This means kittens from the same litter could have a mix of short, long, or no tails at all!

gene—a part of every cell that carries physical and behavioral information passed from parents to their offspring

21

GLOSSARY

ancestor (AN-sess-tur)—a family member who lived a long time ago

claw (KLAW)—a hard, curved nail on the foot of an animal

communicate (kuh-MYOO-nuh-kate)—to pass along thoughts, feelings, or information

depth (DEPTH)—distance from top to bottom or from front to back

domestic (duh-MES-tik)—tame; no longer wild

flexible (FLEK-suh-buhl)—able to bend

gene (JEEN)—a part of every cell that carries physical and behavioral information passed from parents to their offspring

gland (GLAND)—an organ in the body that makes natural chemicals or helps substances leave the body

groom (GROOM)—to clean and make an animal look neat

hairball (HAIR-bawl)—a ball of fur that lodges in a cat's stomach

litter (LIT-ur)—small bits of clay or other material used to absorb the waste of cats and other animals

nurse (NURSS)—to feed young with milk from the mother's body

pitch (PICH)—how high or low a sound is

pupil (PYOO-puhl)—the round, dark center of the eye that lets in light

range (RAYNJ)—the distance from which sound can be heard

routine (roo-TEEN)—a regular way or pattern of doing tasks

sensitive (SENS-i-tiv)—able to feel things easily

solitary (SOL-uh-ter-ee)—living or spending a lot of time alone

territory (TER-uh-tor-ee)—an area of land that an animal claims as its own to live in

vaccination (vak-suh-NAY-shun)—a shot of medicine that protects animals from a disease

veterinarian (vet-ur-uh-NER-ee-uhn)—a doctor who treats sick or injured animals

vibrate (VYE-brate)—to move back and forth quickly

READ MORE

Carney, Elizabeth. *Cats vs. Dogs.* Washington, D.C.: National Geographic, 2011.

Guillain, Charlotte. *Cats.* Animal Family Albums. Chicago: Capstone Raintree, 2013.

Olson, Gillia M. *Pet Cats Up Close.* Pets Up Close. North Mankato, Minn.: Capstone Press, 2015.

INTERNET SITES

FactHound offers a safe, fun way to find Internet sites related to this book. All of the sites on FactHound have been researched by our staff.

Here's all you do:

Visit *www.facthound.com*

Type in this code: 9781491450505

Check out projects, games and lots more at
www.capstonekids.com

Critical Thinking Using the Common Core

1. Name two ways owners care for their cats. Why do you think these jobs are important? (Key Ideas and Details)

2. Name three ways a cat's senses of touch, hearing, sight, and smell help it learn about its world and stay safe. Think of a time when it would have been helpful to have "super senses." How could super senses have helped you? (Integration of Knowledge and Ideas)

INDEX